The Concepts

of

Marriage and Divorce

in the

Hebrew Tradition

Parbar Study Aids: 3

The Concepts

of

Marriage and Divorce

in the

Hebrew Tradition

their growth & development,
to their form at the time of Jesus

David Robertson

Parbar Study Aids: 3

Parbar Publishing

Copyright © David Robertson 1980

Cover Design: © Riach Wilson 2012

First published by Parbar Publishing as an eBook
2012 ASIN: B007PZFHXS

This edition Parbar Publishing 2015
ISBN: 978-1-911018-04-9

Unless otherwise stated, scripture quotations are taken
from the Holy Bible, New International Version
Anglicised Copyright © 1979, 1984, 2011 Biblica, formerly
International Bible Society

Used by permission of Hodder & Stoughton Publishers,
an Hachette UK company.
'NIV' is a registered trademark of Biblica
UK trademark number 1448790.

The New Oxford Annotated Bible with Apocrypha,
Expanded Edition Revised Standard Version),
Oxford University Press, 1977

Contents

Parbar Study Aids

Parbar Publishing

Introduction

I was ordained as a clergyman in the Church of England in 1979 and began working as a curate. Day by day I met people who talked to me about their relationships because they wanted to know how to live these relationships in a Christian way. They told me very personal stories about their sex-lives, their marriages, their joys and their frustrations. They asked me questions and expected me to provide answers, or at the very least suggestions, that would help them.

At that time (in the Church of England), we were being asked to discuss the remarriage of divorcees. I wanted to know what the culture of Jesus' day thought (and taught) on this issue, but I couldn't find a book about it. My post-ordination training required that I study and write an essay so I chose: 'The concepts of marriage and divorce in the Hebrew tradition; their growth and development, to their form at the time of Jesus.'

This provided me with some fundamental understandings, some primary biblical principles, and became a key ingredient in my thinking on the subject of relationships. 25 years later I wrote *Marriage: Restoring Our Vision*. This was published by BRF in 2005 and is now reprinted by Parbar Publishing as a paperback and an eBook.

This *Parbar Study Aid* is the original essay and, therefore, different in style to *Marriage: Restoring Our Vision*. It is offered to students and readers who want to study the various texts for themselves and to chart the development of marriage and divorce in the Old Testament in more detail. References are included in the text and Greek and Hebrew words are italicised and transliterated into English.

David Robertson 2015

The Essay

The Concepts of Marriage and Divorce in the Hebrew Tradition; their growth & development, to their form at the time of Jesus.

Marriage is both a private and a public institution. It is private in that it is a framework within which a most intimate relationship between a man and a woman takes place, and it is public in that it is a 'proclaimed' relationship. As a private relationship, the form reflects the expectations of the individuals. As a public union, it reflects the sociological and cultural expectations of the place and time in which it takes place. In the Hebrew tradition, marriage and its dissolution can be seen to reflect not only personal, social and cultural development, but the attitudes of the 'chosen people' who wish to be formed by their understanding of the expectations of God.

For the Hebrew, sex and religion were always very closely linked; the most obvious example being male circumcision. Although the primitive concept of marriage was, in large part, simply a continuation of the practices of other Near Eastern cultures, there was also a strand of thought that made sex and marriage for the Hebrew rather different. To other Near Eastern cultures, the creation of the world was linked to the procreation of the gods, but to the Hebrew, the creation came into being by God's Word, and sexuality was never directly connected to the creator. No consorts were ever attributed to God, and to be a 'Son of God' was a relational, not sexual, descent. Marriage was therefore regarded as a purely human activity.

In this area of life, as in all others, the Hebrew believed that God required some actions and condemned others. Tracing the course of this developing understanding is no simple matter because the biblical record is, in general, a chronologically later record of the events and practices described. The task of differentiating accurate reporting from 'reading back' (current practices as if they were history), is very difficult. This essay, however, will proceed on the assumption that where practices accord in general with the cultural practices of the time being recorded, they are reasonably accurate.

Primitive Practices

As far as the most primitive forms of marriage are concerned we have no records, but if modern primitive societies offer any parallel, a form of temporary monogamy was probably the rule. There are, however, hints in the biblical narrative as to early practices. In its early form marriage was probably endogenous and similar to the Egyptian and Persian practice where marriage between brothers, sisters and parents was accepted. For example, Abraham is recorded as having married his half sister (Genesis 20:12), Lot's daughters became pregnant through their father (Genesis 19:30-38), Jacob married two sisters, and Moses' father married his own aunt (Exodus 6:20). None of these relationships seems to have met with public disapproval.

The Patriarchal stories show several phases of matrimonial development, and by the time of David, when his son Ammon could have married his half sister Tamar (2 Samuel 13:13), public opinion was definitely against it. It is obvious from the biblical account that family life was frequently less than idyllic, with trouble between husband and wife as well as between the generations; however, from the beginning of the account there is no question but that sex was regarded as residing firmly within the human sphere. Sex was never used to placate or encourage the spirit world, and was regarded as a matter for self-control and an important pointer to the individuality of Man. Thus sex was firmly embedded in human relationships, rather than in forms of worship, and part and parcel of being human.

This was emphasised by the belief that body and soul were united. The soul was not regarded as pre-existent and neither was it thought to survive the body. In Hebrew thinking, people did not *have* bodies, they *were* bodies and so the uses to which the body was put were part and parcel of obedience, or otherwise, to God. Sex was not recognised as sacred in a pagan way, but it was recognised as a powerful force with limits to the appropriate and responsible use of it. Sex was important and therefore largely limited to marriage relationships, with the style of marriage determining the style of the community, and vice-versa.

Some scholars have found evidence in the Old Testament of the remains of an earlier matriarchal style of marriage – a style of marriage in which the figure of authority was the mother. The evidence for this is suggested when the husband settles with the wife's kin, or when the husband returns to the mother's household (as with Jacob and Moses), or when the wife remains at home and the husband visits her (as with Samson). Also, when the wife shows authority (as with Hagar when she takes a wife for her son (see Genesis 21:21), without a challenge from her husband. However, this evidence does not really seem tenable – in Moses' and Jacob's cases their actions were a result of flight, and in Samson's case the fact that his wife lived elsewhere in her own dwelling seems to have more to do with her being a foreigner than a matriarch. Also, although the authority of some of the women, and even their use of separate tents to dwell in, is undisputed, a matriarchal marriage has more to do with line of descent than with personal authority. It is commonly observed that many strong women wield great personal authority from within highly patriarchal societies.

In the Old Testament there is no evidence of descent through the mother's line; quite the contrary, in fact. The line of descent was traced through the father as can be seen by the genealogies in Genesis. Also, by and large, it was the father who named the child (see Genesis 4:26 5:3, 29; 38:3) although the mother sometimes did this (see Genesis 4:25; 29:32-35), and in that naming there was the essence of self-transmission from father to son, continuing the line of the name in a special way. Also, although the mother may have had her own apartment (Judges 15:1; 16:4; 1 Kings 7:8), and managed the household servants (1 Samuel 25:19), it was the father who had absolute authority. This extended to married sons and their wives if they lived with him. In early times this included the power of life and death (Genesis 38:24). The father also had authority over his own wife, and she was in no sense regarded as his equal. She was an object to be acted upon, to be 'taken to wife' (Genesis 20:2-3), and her father and husband determined her marriage and her fate. Indeed, the word 'husband' (*ba'al*) means 'Lord' and although he was not (*adhon*) a 'complete conqueror', his Lordly role was the centre of the strength, foundation and well-being of his family. The wife was owned... and valuable. She was therefore well cared for and not shut away as in some cultures, and had a certain freedom and influence (see: Sarah, Rebekah, Deborah, Jael, Abigail, Athaliah), but she was still owned by her husband.

Interestingly, because of this central role of the husband, polygamy was natural to the Hebrews. The male was central to the family, and he had a religious drive to increase and extend the family. This meant having sons and so polygamy, or more accurately polygyny was common. There was no limit to the number of wives a man might have, except that he must be able to support them. In actual fact, polygyny can only be universal where wives are procured by capture, or when a whole slice of the male population are killed in battle, because there are not, otherwise, enough women for every husband to marry several. Also, on a practical level, it was only the rich who could afford more than one wife.

The earliest Hebrew, Abraham, seems to have been following the custom of the time (the code of Hammurabi c1700BC), which was that a second wife was taken only if the first proved to be barren. On the whole, the patriarchs seem to have been more lax than their Mesopotamian counterparts (for example, Jacob and Esau), when they took more than one wife. It must, however, be remembered that they understood themselves to be building a new nation, and therefore, the more wives, the more children. Also, this was not true of every patriarch; Isaac, for example had only one wife. In practice, we see the Old Testament writers criticising these polygynous marriages when they are recorded as being far from ideal.

Although affection is not limited to one person, in practice there seems always to have been a clear favourite, and the favourite wife was generally the most fertile wife – although this was not universally the case (see Rachel and Hannah). Socially, the barren woman ranked below the fertile slave, and polygyny can be argued to be the result of social pressure rather than personal choice. In many ways, polygyny was more suited to a nomadic existence than to town dwelling – where there was less space.

It is interesting to note that linguistically, the root meaning of the word for 'second wife' is 'to show hostility toward' (Ecclesiasticus 26:6;

1 Samuel 1:6). Thus polygyny resulted, most usually, from a desire for children, more rarely from love or lust (see the stories of David and Bathsheba, Jacob and Rachel), and increasingly, as civilisation developed, from political diplomacy among the rich – for the purpose of securing alliances through blood ties. Monogamy, however, was increasingly held to be the ideal; an ideal which found its fullest expression in the teaching of the prophets. It is probably no accident that characters such as Noah, the 'only righteous man' in the world, are depicted as having a monogamous marriage.

Before the introduction of the law, the rules of 'who not to marry' were very simple: marriage was not permitted to anyone living in the same tent. Thus a certain exogamous principle was the established norm, and endogamy was encouraged within certain limits. The wife was sought from amongst those not removed by racial or cultural barriers, and the natural place to look was amongst cousins (for example, the marriages of Isaac and Jacob). There were of course exceptions – Joseph married an Egyptian (Genesis 41:45), and Moses a Midianite (Exodus 2:21), but these were the result of exceptional circumstances.

In times of comparative peace, wives were taken from within the close family. It was in this way, perhaps more than in any other, that the individuality of the Hebrew race was kept intact – to the extent that later on, much emphasis was placed upon not taking 'foreign wives'. Marriages were arranged by the parents, or more specifically, by the fathers. The father held the family power and it was therefore his task to find spouses for his children. Although this grates with contemporary Western thinking it should be remembered that the children being married were very young, generally at puberty, which would usually be at the age of twelve for a girl and thirteen for a boy (as indeed the Rabbis were later to fix these ages). If the chronology is correct, Joiakin married at sixteen, Ammon and Josias at fourteen, and these marriages may well have been late. The emphasis on marrying the eldest daughter first is also to be understood in this context – the eldest would be eligible for marriage but her younger sisters would still be minors.

In Babylon, a marriage without the consent of the father was invalid, but amongst the Hebrews it was valid – this emphasised the contractual nature of the Hebrew marriage.

Although the father had absolute power, his power rested upon the obedience of those whom he 'ruled.' Thus, he could not, by his word alone, annul a marriage – because it existed, contractually, in its own right. In the normal run of things, the first step towards a marriage would be taken by the suitor's parents (Genesis 24; 34:4-6, Judges 14:2-10), but even so things were socially quite free. The girls did not veil and at harvest festivals and at the well the sexes were free to meet and mingle (Genesis 24:15-20, 29:2-11; Exodus 2:15-19), and it seems that often the two met and formed an attachment (Genesis 29:9-12, 18; 1 Samuel 18:20-27), before the formal suiting began. Thus there is evidence that love as well as arrangement was recognised as a criterion for marriage and the longing of a woman for a man was thought to be determined by God (Genesis 3:16).

To the Hebrew then, marriage was not just a family affair, but important to the individuals, even though the main emphasis rested with the family. The strength and identity of the family depended upon the strength and identity of the marriage. A marriage meant the mixing of families and therefore the respective fathers were anxious to see a suitable match. To the Hebrew it was important that the couple should leave their respective families and begin their own family, but in practical terms it was usually the groom's family that received the bride. The new marriage was identical to the father's marriage, and yet it was different because it extended the family and the wife still had ties with her own family – she was not simply cut off or adopted.

After the first initial contact between the parents, the next step to marriage was the betrothal. This required, first of all, the consent of the parents, and second, the payment of the 'purchase price' (*mohar*) to the girl's family. This could be money, or service in the fields, or service during war (Genesis 29, 1 Samuel 18:25). Once the *mohar* was paid, the two were betrothed and legally man and wife (then, rather than at the marriage), and they could live as man and wife straight away or at a later date (Genesis 24:49-67; Judges 14:5ff). This can be clearly seen where the future sons-in-law of Lot are counted as sons-in-law (Genesis 19:14). It is also probable that in the early stages, betrothal was the time of circumcision, as a joint preparation for marriage and an initiation rite – uniting the spiritual intent of 'God's holy nation' with the practical process of conceiving it. Evidence for this can be seen in the circumcision of Ishmael (Genesis 17:25) at the age of thirteen, and linguistically in that the word for 'father-in-law' means 'circumciser.'

None of these 'transactions' however should be confused with 'marriage by purchase.' Although the woman was an object acted upon by men-folk she was, none the less, a free woman. Slaves were bought and sold, but women were not. The monetary exchanges involved in marriage were more to do with making good the loss of a daughter, or the reward, perhaps, for an acceptance of a proposal (Genesis 24:53), and in fact Genesis 24 pictures a delicate interplay of human relationships rather than bartering or commerce. Similarly, although wives sometimes came from war captives (Judges 5:30; 21:21; Deuteronomy 21:10-14), there was never in the Hebrew concept of marriage any specific 'marriage by capture.' For the Hebrew, marriage was not simple possession, it was an important relationship basic to family life, and even though sons were vital to the marriage it seems to have been recognised (even in the early stages) that it took more than children to produce a happy or satisfactory marriage. Neither was the marriage regarded as a simple transaction – it was something to celebrate.

Exactly how the event was celebrated is not recorded. Evidently Jacob was given a wedding feast and a nuptial week (Genesis 29:20-27), and later writings feature a procession and a feast (Judges 14:10-12; Isaiah 61:10; Jeremiah 2:32). There may also have been a 'skirt covering' ceremony (Ruth 3:9), similar to the Arab practice of throwing the groom's cloak over the bride with the words 'None shall cover you but such a one...' and the name of the groom. The final rite before consummation may well have been proof of virginity – which, incidentally, was not a moral judgement but a proof of paternity with overtones of 'unlawful handling of the goods'. The wife was the property of the husband and therefore sexual violation was a criminal act against the husband.

The Hebrew concept of what was, and what was not, adultery stemmed from the unshakeable position of the husband's centrality to the marriage. As with other primitive codes, adultery ranked in seriousness with murder and was punished severely. In one sense this was to protect the purity and integrity of the clan, but in the emphasised sense it focused upon the violation of another's property. The violation was against the husband, not the wife, and there seems to have been no concept of her willingness or unwillingness; adultery was simply adultery. In its earliest form, the punishment seems to have involved the burning of the woman (Genesis 38:24), but this was later transmuted to stoning. Thus adultery tended to be a double standard – the wife sinned against her husband, but the husband who committed adultery sinned against another man (against the husband of the adulterous woman). There was, therefore, no such thing as adultery with an unmarried person (unless betrothed: in which case it was identical to the violation of marriage), and the seduction of a virgin required her marriage to the man (Exodus 22:16).

In cases where there was suspicion of adultery, there was a trial by ordeal for the wife which was probably taken from Canaanite practice. The trial was, by comparison with other cultures, reasonably clement. It involved the placing of temple dust in a cup, her consumption of the resulting liquid, followed by observation to see if she vomited. Women with a clear conscience probably passed the test. As far as the man was concerned, however, neither polygyny nor the taking of concubines was thought to be adultery.

In real terms, concubinage took the place of adoption and it was evidently encouraged by barren wives (see Sarah and Hagar). As in Babylonian culture, the position of the concubine was protected. Through coitus with her master she was elevated to a status where her children would share in the inheritance of her master/husband (Genesis 21:10). Although the law of Exodus 21:7-11 takes for granted that slaves would naturally become the concubines of the master or of his sons, it would be a mistake to think of this as a product of 'lust' – it had much more to do with the production of children and the fact that anyone wealthy enough to have slaves would probably be wealthy enough to support concubines satisfactorily.

This concept of non-sexual morality within sexual relationships cannot be overemphasised. The sexual-moral sense took a definite back seat to another, far stronger moral sense – the continuation of the family. This can be seen most clearly in the Levirate rule. This rule was that if two brothers lived on the same estate and one died childless, it was then the duty of the survivor to have sons by the widow. In this case, any son resulting from the union would inherit his dead 'father's' property and also continue his name. This rule cut across the endogamy code, and there was no question of adultery. To fail to fulfil this duty was seen as a grave crime (Genesis 38) and although some have seen the remnants of fratriarchal marriage in this practice, it simply serves to emphasise the morality of the time – a morality in which property and the extension of the family were the prime concern. Yet, even with this concern for the estate, it was still within the husband's power to end his marriage at any time that he chose. In Arab tribal practice, the husband needed only to lead his wife to the door of his tent and tell her go to be divorced. The Hebrew had similar power; his wife had no rights and he could dismiss her for any reason he wished.

The Yahwist Strand 'J'

Even at a primitive stage, the rules and traditions governing marriage were complex. It was not until around 950BC with the 'J' creation narrative that there was any formal attempt to explain the order of things – where power was distributed to the man, the provider for his dependant wife. The 'J' narrative (Genesis 2), describes the creation of the male first, from dust... or 'the stuff of creation.' The creation of the female is described as a much more elaborate action. She is described as a 'helper fit for him', (by tradition a 'helpmeet'), although the term really has more of the meaning of 'alongside and corresponding to.' The woman was, in other words, a similar, not just complementary, counterpart, and it is only after the fall that the woman is seen as subordinate. Although it was widely believed that the second creation (the woman) was an inferior one (to the man), in actual fact it is the man (in his solitary insufficiency) who is described as inferior until the creation of the woman. Thus the relationship is depicted as important, even though it was through this relationship that the fall came about, and the purpose of 'J' seems to be to explain the origin of the sexes and their drive for union.

The fall itself is not depicted as a sexual fall. The knowledge of good and evil becomes the possession of man and that to have this knowledge is to 'be like God' (Genesis 3:5). Once the man and the woman have that knowledge, they have 'become like... us [God] ', (Genesis 3:22). As has already been described, God was not regarded as a 'sexual' God and so it is a very unlikely interpretation that the discovery of sex has made the couple 'like God.' Similarly, although the words 'ashamed' and 'naked' are used to describe the couple's reaction to their disobedience, these words have more the meanings of 'conscious' and 'exposed weakness' than any sexual connotation. In fact, S. Sapp in 'Sexuality, the Bible and Science (page 19)' points out that in our own language we have an almost exactly similar phrase which carries this meaning of nakedness, weakness and exposure – we call it 'being caught with your trousers down.'

It is also interesting to note that according to 'J' the fall was a united fall. It was not until both the woman and the man had eaten the forbidden fruit that the eyes of both were opened. This narrative, then, attempts to explain the created, and fallen, order of things, but makes few judgements – and the rules were left to the Deuteronomists.

The Deuteronomist 'D'

The Deuteronomic codes were formed around 600 BC and were not concerned with morality per se, but with the law. They contain no suggestion that sex, in itself, is in any way wrong, and neither do they emphasise sexual sin. Sexual sin is a sin like any other sin, in that it damages the relationship with God and relationships with other people. The codes were concerned with the interpretation of commandments, and within these commandments, sexual sin offended either the cultic purity of the Hebrew people or the procreative system. The seriousness of these offences can be seen in the requirement of the death penalty for adultery and the exclusion of 'the offspring of forbidden marriages' from the 'assembly of the Lord' up to the tenth generation (Deuteronomy 23:2).

The primitive traditions were taken and formalised so that the husband was firmly entrenched as the central figure. Marriage was obligatory, and while there could be widows, there was no such thing as a spinster. On the male side, the only celibates were the 'unable', the mutilated, or the eunuchs (Deuteronomy 23:1). So important were children that exception from military service was allowed to the newlywed for one year (Deuteronomy 20:7, 24:25). It was recognised that the relationship was an intimate one and the exception was also made with regard to the happiness of the couple. Again, the importance of family can be seen in the continuation of the Levirate rule (Deuteronomy 25:5-6), which still took precedence over kindred laws. Now, however, the brother-in-law who does not obey the Levirate rule is open to public disgrace (Deuteronomy 25:7-10), and the concept is one of not only denying the widow but denying the whole line of descent. In the same way the practices of concubinage and polygyny were affirmed and strengthened although an attempt was made to correct abuses – for example the code ruled that the father should acknowledge the first born son even though he may be born to a disliked wife (Deuteronomy 21:15-17). Also, the monarchy and town life had loosened the close knit nomadic family ties and the code attempted to curb the multiplication of the king's wives in order to guard against 'his heart being led astray' (Deuteronomy 17:17), because marriage in the Deuteronomic codes was as intimate as it had been in the primitive codes and it was recognised that harems killed intimacy.

In the Deuteronomic codes, marriage was still very much the prerogative of the family and, as such, arranged by them. The marriage relationship itself was also important in its own right, and the relationship by marriage held exactly the same bond as a relationship by blood. Marriages, or the barring of relationships within the family, were now made plain and marriages with step-mothers, half-sisters and mothers-in-law were added to the list of forbidden relationships – which already contained siblings, parents or offspring (Deuteronomy 22:30; 27:20-23). Also, the fear of marriage to aliens was formalised and forbidden (Deuteronomy 7:1-4), although the act of coitus with a captive was regarded as an act of marriage (Deuteronomy 21:10-14), even though the woman could then be sent away.

In many ways, then, marriage was made more permanent and steps were taken to protect the women – who had few rights. Up until the Deuteronomic reform, women had not been subject to criminal law, but now they became equal members of the covenant community and were held to be guilty of their own indiscretions. Thus, for adultery, the proscribed punishment was stoning, and the husband no longer had the discretion to divorce or forgive his wife. The test of innocence was continued, but with the addition that should she prove herself innocent, then her husband may never divorce her (Deuteronomy 22:13-21). Adultery was a sin because the woman was her husband's possession, and it was an affront to him because paternity was in doubt and his line of descent threatened. There was still no distinction between voluntary and involuntary adultery and the rules sought to protect not only the husband, but, to some extent, the wife who was innocent and wrongly accused. Similarly, sexual offences were now no longer a question of personal revenge, but matters to be dealt with by officers of the law – again to protect the innocent. The codes also removed the right of a father to keep a seduced daughter as well as any money or damages (Deuteronomy 22:28-29), which points towards a closer linking of sex and marriage than was previously the norm. However, it should be noted that, even in these codes, extra-marital sex was not forbidden – it was a question of damages rather than morality.

As far as divorce was concerned, the husband was still absolute master and could divorce his wife if: 'he finds something indecent about her' (Deuteronomy 24:1), which was very vague and caused much discussion later on. However, an important check upon hasty or unjust divorce was the necessity of obtaining a writ of divorce (Deuteronomy 24:1-3), which allowed the woman to remarry. This writ provided a check in two ways. First, writing was not a usual skill that most people possessed, so the husband had to persuade a scribe to write it for him. The time needed to compose, write, collect and deliver the writ provided time to consider. Second, the scribe consulted was not only a legal expert but also an advisor – and therefore, to obtain the writ of divorce, the husband would of necessity come under the supervision of another and, perhaps, helpful individual.

Whether a wife could divorce her husband is less clear. General wisdom states that she could not, but this may not have been the case throughout the Diaspora. Amongst the papyri discovered at Elphantine (a Hebrew colony in Egypt from the 5th century BC), a marriage contract has been found where the wife has the right to divorce her husband: 'if tomorrow or any later day Miphtahyah shall stand up in the congregation and say "I divorce As-Hor, my husband," the price of divorce shall be on her head...if tomorrow or any later time As-Hor shall stand up in the congregation and say" 'I divorce my wife, Miphtahyah," her marriage settlement shall be forfeited.' Whether this example of the wife having the right to institute divorce is a singular exception or a reflection of a common pattern, is simply not known. Deuteronomically, only divorce writs are mentioned, not marriage contracts, and so it is assumed that this practice was not widespread within Israel itself. There were certain cases where a wife could demand a divorce from her husband, but even then the actual power of divorce was his, and the only cases where he could not divorce his wife were where he had seduced and married a virgin or had falsely accused his wife of adultery (Deuteronomy 22:13-19, 28-29). It was also now forbidden to remarry a previously divorced wife of one's own (Deuteronomy 24:1-4), and although the codes took pains to designate what could and could not happen, the interest was purely legal, not social, and the divorced wife was left to fend for herself. This meant returning to her family and then remarrying.

There is no Deuteronomic ruling with regard to alimony or possession of children (who presumably stayed with the father). Again, it cannot be emphasised too strongly that the Deuternomic codes were interested in the legal application of the Hebrew tradition and not at all in its moral basis.

The Prophets

The moral sense to marriage developed under the prophets. They believed that all sin was a repudiation of Yahweh and therefore a threat to the covenant relationship between Him and Israel. Previously, the relationship between a man and his wife had been recognised, but now it was emphasised and encouraged. The term 'to know' had always been used as a euphemism for sex, but under the prophets it took on the added meaning of intimate knowledge in more than the sexual sense – not that the meaning had been absent before, but the prophets majored on it. Marriage was now seen as a personal, social and spiritual relationship and love was urged (Proverbs 5:19).

The purpose of marriage was seen in the idea that children were the completion of the creation (Isaiah 45:18), 'He did not create it to be empty, but formed it to be inhabited.' Now, though, in spite of the concern to fulfil God's creation, the drive to produce children did not extend to polygyny. The prophets discouraged polygyny and monogamy was presented as the original and ideal state. Plurality of wives first appeared amongst the Canaanites (Genesis 4:19-24), and was represented as a style of marriage not originally intended by God. Hosea and Isaiah each had only one wife and the discouragement of polygyny was directed mostly towards the monarch. From Samuel to 2 kings, the period covering the monarchy, there is only one recorded commoner who had more than one wife, (Samuel's father right at the start of the narrative), and the kings were rebuked for expedient marriages (1 Kings 11:1-6, 16:31-33). Hand in hand with this prohibition, there were laws against intermarriage that were probably not earlier that the late prophetic codes (Exodus 34:15-16, Deuteronomy 7:1-4), which were overshadowed by the Babylonian exile and the fear of losing cultural identity. David, Solomon, Ahab, Samson and Ruth were all married to foreigners and all were criticised by later writers – but not by earlier ones. Elijah, though, was strict on intermarriage, and in the shadow of Babylonia the prophets told Israel to put away their foreign wives (so they had evidently taken them with no antisocial pressure) because they were 'doing all this terrible wickedness and are being unfaithful to our God' (Nehemiah 13:23-27).

The most interesting and novel concept concerning marriage which is seen in the prophetic teaching, is their use of marriage in a figurative sense. Deutero-Isaiah, Jeremiah, Ezekiel and Hosea all use marriage to describe the relationship between Israel and God (Isaiah 54:5-6, 62:4-5; Jeremiah 2:2, 3:8, 20; Ezekiel 16:8; Hosea 1-3). The picture is of God's purposeful and persistent love, of his rejoicing over his 'bride'; of a permanent relationship between them. God takes and jealously loves his 'wife' (*one* wife) and the harlotous (apostate) Israel is sent away by God with her writ of divorce – but God is willing to accept the repentant wife back.

The image evidently derived from the prophets' own experience of marriage and of their expectations of that relationship. At the time it would have been a particularly powerful image because it could be set within the background of Canaanite cult prostitution and so forth. The emphasis was upon the 'One God', with the permanent, loving, faithful relationship between that God and his people. The image speaks of a particularly high view of the archetypal marriage. Not surprisingly, the divorce law was also slightly modified. Although divorce was still accepted without question (Hosea 2:2 provides a simple form of the divorce writ (*get*)... 'She is not my wife, I am not her husband'), a divorced wife could be reinstated if she had not remarried (Isaiah 54:6). This was against the Deuteronomic law (Deuteronomy 24:1-4), and Hosea himself broke the law by taking back his unfaithful wife. Thus the emphasis was upon relationship, (upon the making, breaking and repair of the relationship), rather than upon the legalities.

This prophetic teaching found its way into the formal interpretation of law as 'the holiness code'. The fundamental idea was that marriage was given by God and children were a gift and a joy (Psalm 127:3-5, 128:3-6). In the endogamous marriage, the brother's wife was added to the prohibited list along with the stepmother, step-sister, grand-daughter, aunt and daughter-in-law (Leviticus 18:16-25), which caused some conflict later because it contradicted the Levirate rule. This high view of marriage was echoed particularly in the rules governing the marriages of priests: they must not marry an immoral woman, and the wife of the high priest must now be a virgin, not even a widow (Leviticus 21:7-15). It must not be thought, however, that the prophetic teaching was a complete reversal of established custom. The man was still central and all powerful with the right to divorce, and although it is indicated that divorce rather than death was encouraged as the punishment for adultery (Jeremiah 3:8), the actual process of divorce in these circumstances was certainly humiliating for the wife (if Hosea 2:9-10 is any guide, Gomer was stripped and cast out of the house to show that she was no longer provided for).

In the teaching of the Prophets, there was a search for a standard of morality. With this teaching, the making of a marriage had become something more special and something to celebrate, while the breaking of marriage had become something to mourn.

The Priestly Code 'P'

The 'holiness code' was taken and extended by the 'Priestly code' which read back into the text the ideas of the time (these were later 'smoothed out' by successive generations of scribes of the Priestly school. It is difficult to tell what was original and what was not). The 'P' account of Genesis found its final form some time after the exile, around 500BC, and whereas the 'J' account simply recorded the fruitfulness of Adam and Eve, in 'P' fruitfulness was made into a command. To some extent the 'P' source tends to find sex more easily acceptable than 'J' – probably as a result of diminishing pressure from such forms of worship as fertility cults. In 'P', mankind is created 'male and female' and 'Adam' is a generic name (mankind as distinct from animal). Thus both male and female are created together (Genesis 1:27; 5:1-2), without temporal or ontological superiority. In this account of creation, sex is part of God's plan, and both male and female are commanded to 'be fruitful and multiply'. This command is repeated after the flood (Genesis 9:1) and also used as a blessing for achievement (Genesis 12:2, 17:2-6, 22:17).

This concept of procreation as both a command and blessing supports the view that sex and marriage were part of Gods intended creation, rather than as a punishment for sin. This, then, reflects the concept of a time when the major goal in the life of the Hebrew was the propagation of the Hebrew race. It also indicates a very high doctrine of mankind, where both male and female are made 'in the image of God' (Genesis 1:27). The word used for 'image' shows that what was in mind had more to do with capacity and quality than with physiology. This is something of a departure from the non-distinction between body and soul; mankind is now seen as 'spiritually' a reflection of God (like God), yet still a physical being (unlike God). This physical being has a need for sex and marriage and this relationship is regarded as right and proper to such a being. This concept is not highly developed, but it is present.

With such a high doctrine of humanity and sexual relationships, one would expect to find in the Priestly code every encouragement towards the fidelity of husband and wife – and that is exactly what is found. The Priestly code took and formalised the concerns of the prophetic lawgivers, (their concerns about social immorality, which in this context, includes the neglect of marriage vows) and the discouragement of divorce. The wife, through child-bearing and raising, assisted her husband in his duty to God. She created the home and so she may not, by law, evade him. There is no express forbidding of either polygyny or divorce, but the background of 'monogamy as ideal' is plain and every effort is made to make divorce difficult.

The divorce '*get*' was a continued necessity and now a divorced wife could not be taken back – this was to try to discourage hasty divorces. The test for adultery was continued (Numbers 5:12-31), and the punishment severe (Leviticus 19:20-22). Leviticus 21:9 records that a priest's daughter who turned to prostitution was burnt alive; but whether this was an exception because of the priestly family is hard to say. It is, however, worth noting that the thinking behind prohibited marriages (of family members) was connected with the idea that one could not marry oneself, and, for example, one's daughter was a product of oneself, so the action taken upon the daughter of a priestly family may have been about a perceived affront to the priesthood rather than a comment on her personal actions.

The Priestly code, though, was not a complete reversal of tradition. Women had a higher place in this doctrine, but in real life the authority of the husband was as strong, if not stronger, than ever. According to the supplemental Priestly codes, a man had the authority to annul any vow made by his wife (Numbers 30:6-8, 13-15), and the Priestly writers were as caught up in their own time as anyone else. Their major 'problem' was with alien marriages. The people's reaction to exile, and the resulting mixed marriages, led to the rule that such marriages must be punished by the death penalty (Numbers 25:6-13). It is also no surprise, in view of the commandment to extend the nation, that the Levirate rule was still accepted.

The Priestly code substantially developed the doctrine of mankind. This doctrine, aligned with the corresponding development in the Hebrew concept of marriage, was complemented by the wisdom literature.

Wisdom Literature

Wisdom Literature was produced in the post-exilic period and came into its full strength in the inter-Testamental period. As such it gives the final reflections on the concepts of marriage and divorce before the beginning of the New Testament era. Proverbs 5:18-19 sums up the main idea:

'*May your fountain be blessed, and may you rejoice in the wife of your youth. A loving doe, a graceful deer – may her breasts satisfy you always, may you ever be captivated by her love.*'

In Wisdom literature, monogamy was seen as the ideal (Proverbs 31:10), and loyalty to the husband by the wife was much praised. Similarly, fidelity in the husband was highly esteemed and sexual licence regarded as foolish and even fatal. As far as Wisdom was concerned, adultery led to death and the emphasis was upon that death being a moral perdition (Proverbs 2:16-18, 5:3-6, 7:10, 26-27). In Wisdom, the concept is of love within marriage. It is specifically encouraged (Proverbs 5:19), and also by general example – for example, the love between the sexes described in the Song of Songs. By now the idea of marriage by purchase was quite untenable and the family involvement in the arrangement of marriage had begun to take the shape of a covenant relationship (see Proverbs 2:17 and also Malachi 2:14 where the word 'covenant' is used for 'marriage'). Polygyny was never mentioned at all, and although it was not expressly forbidden, the focus was upon exulting in the wife, rather than *wives*, and of the individual home (Proverbs 3:10; 12:4; 18:22; 19:14; Ecclesiasticus 25:1, 8; 26:1, 13).

Wisdom Literature explores the relational aspect of marriage in a new way. It seems to reach the conclusion that it is only within a monogamous framework that the very best can blossom.

The Rabbis: 1st Century AD

Wisdom Literature was at its peak during the inter-Testamental period. By the first century AD the official line was far more legalistic. The sources which reflect the concepts and practices at the time of Jesus can be found in the Midrash. This was collected from the first to the third centuries AD, and also in the Rabbinical debates of the time.

In Jesus' time women, like slaves, were pledged to observe all the negative prohibitions of the law, but they were not expected to keep all the positive commands. This was because they were subject to their husband's rule of law; for the wife, the husband was her law. That women followed Jesus must have been an anathema to the strict Jews of the day, for in that world women had a choice of only two careers – wife or prostitute. Rabbinic thought revolved around the specific exegesis of Biblical Law rather than around moral concepts, and Jesus would have been regarded as having no business teaching this to women.

In practice, marriage was still similar to the inherited culture. Children still married young, with the usual arrangement at betrothal of an agreed marriage portion being given to the bride, a dowry given to the husband and a marriage settlement for the wife in the event of divorce or the death of the husband. Marriage was still obligatory and it was the duty of the spouse to remarry after divorce or the death of a partner. The sexes could still mix freely, but the number of social opportunities where they could meet were now limited, in order to cut down infidelity. The exact nature, however, of what was practiced in ordinary families in the first century is far from clear. Records tend to relate to the 'ruling classes' rather than to 'the common herd' and it is only in later writings that we find any accurate reflection of the accepted norm.

Divorce at this period was a moot point, but the subject was under discussion by two major schools of thought. The origin of the husband's right to divorce his wife was found in the Patriarchal family (Genesis 21:9-14), and the basic concept was not in dispute. The causes, however, were. The Shammai school held that there could be no divorce without cause and that the cause could only be sexual immorality. The Hillel school held that a husband could divorce his wife for any reason at all. Owing to public opinion, the Hillel school was accepted (!), although it is evident from the Gospels that Jesus agreed with the Shammai school. Each Rabbinic school accepted divorce (and therefore remarriage) – the disagreement was over cause, and therefore the state of the subsequent marriage. For the Hillel school, any reason would do. For the Shammai school, sexual immorality was the only acceptable cause, and the teaching can be summed up as: *if a partner commits adultery (or sexual immorality), the law requires the death penalty; however, we no longer carry out that penalty, instead we permit divorce; the remaining partner, may then, regard the penalty as carried out and is free to remarry without taint.* It is from this direction that Jesus is coming when he speaks of divorce and remarriage in Matthew 5:31-32.

The Mishnah added three restrictions: divorce could not be granted on the grounds of insanity, or where the partner had been captured and removed, or where a minor was involved. The bureaucracy was also increased to try to make divorce more difficult and to ensure that marital difficulties came under the scrutiny of the authorities. It was also established that a wife could demand a '*get*' from her husband in certain circumstances and sometimes the courts stepped in and compelled separation. Even so, a wife could not actually divorce her husband, only demand that he divorce her; Salome, the sister of Herod tried, but her action was held to be against Jewish Law. So, by this time the civil courts took a far greater part in family life than before, even to the extent of deciding upon custody of the children in cases of divorce.

The concept of marriage was still unmistakably an extension of the commandment to 'be fruitful and multiply.' Neither the ascetic trends of Pharisaic Judaism nor any other movement advocated celibacy, and it was very rare to find any 'un-mutilated' person in that state (*see page 23; refer to Deuteronomy 23:1*). The focus was upon marrying young and the courts could, in fact, force anyone over twenty to marry. Late marriage was often a sign of poor social status, but to be unmarried was to be 'one who... [is] ... without good, and without a helper, and without joy, and without a blessing, and without atonement' (R. Jacob). Another Rabbi said that such a man was not a whole man, and others that an unmarried man diminished God's likeness (this is an extension of the 'P' concept of creation. It states that it is the man and woman *together* who form the image of God – therefore the unmarried are less than the image). Simeon ben 'Azzai (who, incidentally, was unmarried himself), went as far as to say that an unmarried man was like one who shed blood (i.e. the blood of the unconceived children).

After divorce, remarriage was expected, although a period of three months was required to ensure that there would be no confusion over the paternity of subsequent children. Similarly, remarriage was expected from the widow or widower, and the rule of two witnesses to attest death was dropped in favour of one to allow the widow to remarry more easily. Thus, although it was accepted that marriage ended at death, remarriage could only take place after legal proof of that death. This emphasis on marriage and the bearing of children meant that the barren, or unmarried, were social outcasts, and there were certain occupations prohibited to the unmarried – for example, the teaching of children.

The drive to extend the race did not continue into the realms of polygyny. Under the Roman Empire, monogamy was the rule. There was no specific prohibition of polygyny in the law (as there is not for the general population in the New Testament), but it was, however, discouraged. Later on, the Talmud fixed the number of wives at 18 for the king and four for his subjects, but poverty, and public opinion, ensured that monogamy was the general rule. The Levirate rule was still enforced, but by this time, the '*halitzah*' (the ceremony that publicly disgraced the man who did not obey the Levirate rule), was regarded as a socially acceptable alternative to the Levirate union and the Rabbis encouraged men to go through the '*halitzah*' instead. The Rabbis also ensured that the dominant position of the husband was enforced, and although there is some evidence that husbands shared in some of the household tasks (for example, the weekly bread-making was a job for the whole family), even for a rich wife it was an 'anger and impudence and great reproach' that she should keep her husband (Ecclesiasticus 25:22). Wifely duties were confined to the household and it was the duty of the husband to be the provider. This subjection of women was often 'proved' by the popular, but erroneous, etymology of the words for 'man' and 'woman' (*'esh*' and *'esha*'). These words were regarded as proof that a woman was made from a man and therefore inferior (although, in actual fact, the roots of these two words are entirely different and the similarity of sounds is no more than an accidental pun).

Legalistic though the first century concepts of marriage were, there was room for a certain aesthetic approach. The anathema of being unmarried has already been mentioned and there was a genuine belief that married life was the most natural expression of creation. Arranged marriages of minors were discouraged by setting the lower age limit at twelve for a girl and thirteen for a boy, and it was clearly expected that marriage should produce not only children but happiness. It was believed that marriages were planned by God forty days before birth, that marriages were 'made in heaven' and that this task was as difficult for God as dividing the Red Sea for Moses and the people!

Marriage was important enough for a man to sell a scroll of the law in order to provide money for a marriage, and the choice of a wife was regarded as very important: 'Hasten to buy land; deliberate before taking a wife.' (Yev. 63 a). No one should marry above himself; 'A shoe that is longer than my foot I do not desire.' (Kid 49a), but a good and virtuous wife was regarded as a great blessing – even though beauty (and even similarity of stature) was regarded as favourable. The ceremony itself was held in reverence and called '*kiddushin*', meaning 'sanctification', and the wife was regarded as sacred and prohibited to all but her husband. This understanding of marriage allowed the continued use of marriage as a picture to express the relationship between God and his people, and, later on, it was also taken as a picture of the relationship between Israel and the Torah. The Torah was thus sanctified to Israel and prohibited to other nations. These concepts were very much in tune with monogamy, and under the new social pressures, concubinage did not make much of an impression, (as much as anything due to the fact that Hebrew slaves were unlikely to work in Hebrew households), and although adultery was still regarded as very serious, the death penalty was no longer enforced and divorce generally replaced it.

As with all Hebrew Law, the form that marriage and divorce took in the first century AD was highly complex. The basic concepts behind those laws, however, were not. Marriage was regarded as God-given; both a blessing and a commandment within which great happiness and love could be found as well as obligatory duties. That marriages did break down was accepted and divorce was acceptable, with the further expectation of remarriage. Throughout the Hebrew tradition, the understanding of the marriage relationship is as a reflection of the understanding of man and his relationship with God, and it is a tradition that Jesus himself took and extended during his ministry. Marriage was seen as an important part of creation and perhaps it is worth repeating that to the first century Hebrew, it was only when a man and a woman were united in this relationship that they could be described as fulfilling their intended, created purpose, of being 'in the image of God.'

If you have found this Study Aid helpful, please leave a review. This will enable other readers to find this essay more easily. Thank you.

Bibliography

S. Sapp. *Sexuality, the Bible and science*. Fortress Press. Philadelphia 1977

J. Pederson. *Israel, Life and Culture*. Oxford University Press. London 1926

A. Bertholet. *A History of Hebrew Civilisation*. George G Harrap & Co Ltd. London 1926

J.L. Crenshaw & J.T. Willis. *Essays in O.T. Ethics*. KTAV Publ. House Inc. New York 1974

C.F. Kent. *Israel's Laws and Legal Precedents*. Hodder & Stoughton. London 1920

A. Phillips. *Ancient Israel's Criminal Law*. Basil Blackwell. Oxford 1970

I. Singer. *The Jewish Encyclopaedia vol 3*. Funk & Wagnalls Co. London 1904

J. Hastings. *Encyclopaedia of Religion and ethics vol 8*. T.T.Clark. Edinburgh 1915

The interpreters Dictionary of the Bible vols 1, 3, 4. Abingdon Press. New York 1962

J.B. Bauer. *Encyclopaedia of Biblical Theology vol 2*. Sheed & Ward Ltd. London 1970

W. Forster. *Palestinian Judaism in N.T. Times.* Oliver & Boyd Ltd. London 1964

S. Schechter. *Studies in Judaism.* Adam & Charles Black. London 1908

G.F. Moore. *Judaism in the first centuries of the Christian Era, the age of Tannain vols 1 & 2.* Harvard University Press. Harvard 1927

S. Safrai & M. Stern. *The Jewish People in the first century vols 1&2* Fortress Press. Philadelphia 1976

H. Danby (Translator) *The Mishnah.* Oxford university Press. London 1933

H. Polano (Translator) *The Talmud.* Frederick Warne & Co. London

R. de Vaux. *Ancient Israel, its Life and Institutions.* Darton Longman & Todd. London 1961

The report of the General Synod Marriage Commission. *Marriage & the Church's task.* CIO Publ. London 1978

More Parbar Study Aids

Christian Witness

to the gospel of peace
in a culture of conflict

RS Robertson

This academic dissertation examines the tension between witness to a gospel of peace and the conflict that arises as a direct result of that witness, and unpacks the thinking behind peaceable witness as an individual and as a community. It provides an overview of theological thought, engages with the contemporary situation, and is offered for the use of students and thinkers who wish to consider this subject in an academic way.

About the Author

RS Robertson graduated from Edinburgh University in 2008 with a first class degree in Divinity. She contributed to 'communities of peaceable difference' in Lebanon, India and South Africa and is now based in the United Kingdom where she works as a professional musician.

Also by David Robertson

David Robertson writes both nonfiction and fiction under his own name, and fiction in different genres under the pen names of JB Duncan and Riach Wilson.

He is the vicar of a busy parish in West Yorkshire, England, the son of an internationally known musician, the husband of a wonderful wife and the father of four adult children. Before ordination he worked in a variety of 'ordinary' jobs, some of which sound quite exotic – such as working in a bamboo factory – but the reality was much more mundane (the bamboo factory, for example, manufactured drain rods).

He is interested in most things and enjoys reading and writing in different genres.

Collaborative Ministry

What it is, how it works, & why

Collaborative Ministry is fast becoming a 'buzz phrase' in the church, following on from phrases such as 'every member ministry' and 'the priesthood of all believers'. It is referred to by those who speak and write about leadership, the Church and outreach, but what exactly does it mean? And does it fit with existing leadership structures?

This book comprehensively explores the theology and practice of this style of 'being church', considering the implications for churches both large and small. A central section provides foundational Bible studies, unpacking the themes of authority, acceptance and covenant, while an appendix of group study material offers help for churches considering a collaborative approach.

Marriage; Restoring our Vision

This book aims to restore our vision of God's created purpose for marriage. It allows the Bible to shed light on both our inherited cultural values and our contemporary Christian assumptions. Linking with the vows in the Marriage Service, it examines biblical principles and challenges current practice. The book also unpacks difficult issues such as cohabitation, divorce and remarriage.

Entertaining, thought provoking and stimulating, this book can be read by an individual, used as the basis for a Bible study group or as the foundation for a teaching series. The ideas and images used will communicate clearly to young and old, whether single, married or divorced. For all those wanting to think about the subject, it will help them to discover God's pattern for married life.

What Would Jesus Post?

A biblical approach to online interaction

If Jesus had access to the internet, what would he post? And, as importantly, what wouldn't he post? This book asks intriguing questions of those who engage with the internet; which biblical principles inform its use, and how might Christians steward their online presence?

Through reflecting on online engagement we can establish good principles for online interaction. For adults, children and young people, and ideal for parents, leaders and ministers, home groups and youth pastors.

Fiction ~ David Robertson

KALEB's TESTIMONY

Christian Oblate Zombie Hunters: Book 1

Kaleb is 20, an Oblate of Trinity Cloister, London, and a member of the Watch. His duties are to dispatch the Scourge (the walking-dead), and report on Pestilents (the living-dead). His fear is their 'Judas kiss' by which all flesh is betrayed, so don your armour with prayer, draw your sword, and join him; but be of good comfort: 'Thou shalt be hid from the scourge of the tongue: neither shalt thou be afraid of pestilence when it cometh.' Job 5:21.

Available as eBooks:

BIBLE INSIGHT STORIES
Zack's Difficult Day

Shammai Shares His Supper

Deborah's Denarius

Manny's Missing Mutton

TELL IT AGAIN STORIES
Bertie's Quest for the Perfect Pearl

Fiction ~ JB Duncan

The Holy Rude Diaries combine down-to-earth humour with a hint of the numinous. They are quintessentially British, with British spelling, British idiom and understated British humour - but Glossaries are provided for readers unfamiliar with the terms used.

THE CURATE OF COCKLEIGH

A tale of Anglicans, Angels & Arson

In 1977, Rev John Davidson is the newly ordained Curate of Cockleigh. His ministry is quite ordinary until he meets an anarchist and begins to see angels…

As he navigates his way around mistaken identity, a vindictive detective, a teenager with romance on her mind and a septuagenarian Kung-Fu Rector, his life becomes a frantic rollercoaster ride towards an explosive conclusion.

The Curate of Cockleigh is clever, outrageous, insightful, provocative and very funny.

THE VICAR OF WESTFEIL

A tale of Faith, Farce & Felony

As the millennium approaches and the banks are exploiting the public, St Jude's Church in Westfeil is quietly exploiting the banks. Faced with an enormous repair bill, the Vicar of Westfeil, Rev John Davidson, initiates a scheme that will fund the repairs. The scheme is ingenious, highly successful and has just one, minor problem; it is also completely illegal...

Set against the background of this fund-raising scheme, The Vicar of Westfeil follows the maverick ministry of John Davidson and the fortunes of the people of Westfeil as they move from failure to crowning success.

The Vicar of Westfeil is honest, moving, sly, scurrilous, challenging and, as always, very funny.

THE BISHOP OF BANFORD

A tale of Crosiers, Cherubs & Crime

Maverick vicar, John Davidson, the new Bishop of Banford, is plunged headlong into a diocesan world of relentless work, financial anxiety, repressed sexuality and inspired lunacy. His marriage begins to fall apart, an old flame reignites and unseen enemies move against him. He is forced to consider hard choices – but then he comes to the unwelcome attention of a crime-lord and finally experiences the most terrifying meeting of his life.

The Bishop of Banford is complex, mischievous, astute, compassionate and, of course, very funny.

Amazon Reviews:

'A good read.'

'The Bishop continues to delight us with his heartfelt efforts to do what is right but continues to stumble over his own feet... This third book in the series is also very funny.'

A PAIR OF SHORTS

Two novellas in one volume: *The St Jude's Shuffle* and *Not a Leg to Stand On*. Both are available, individually as eBooks but are published in *A Pair of Shorts* in one paperback volume.

THE ST JUDE'S SHUFFLE

A Tale of Decision, Deceit & Dysentery

With clergy interviews, a clandestine fund-raising scheme, a conceited Archdeacon, an uncandid candidate, multiple hidden agendas, devious church members and something nasty lurking in the parish buffet, *The St Jude's Shuffle* follows the fortunes of Westfeil church as they hunt for a new Vicar.

The St Jude's Shuffle is empathetic, honest, intelligent and as readers have come to expect, very funny.

Amazon Reviews:

'Funny, gossipy and true to life.'

NOT A LEG TO STAND ON

A Tale of Pretence, Pride & Paradox

Rev. Canon Austen Pillinger, Bishop's Chaplain, has lost his faith, embezzled diocesan funds and is on the run from a vicious loan-shark. Suicide seems to be his only option until a strange dream promises to change his life forever...

Not A Leg To Stand On is mischievous, intelligent and subtle, and will delight readers who enjoy the piquant taste of black humour.

Available as an eBook

AN APTITUDE FOR AVARICE

A Tale of Perfidy, Posing & Pensions

When antiques dealer Barry Salterton visits a downsizing elderly couple, he cannot believe his luck! Their home is stuffed with treasures and Barry is just the man to take them off their hands. His eye is drawn to a particularly rare and beautiful clock – but as negotiations begin, the deal becomes much less straightforward than Barry hoped...

Fiction ~ Riach Wilson

ABOUT THE SERIES

Every novel in the *Boxed In* series is an independent story in its own right and the series can be read in any order. Each novel is told from the viewpoint of the main character who is, in some way, 'boxed in'. Some characters also appear in other novels – which allows the reader to see them in a different light. Across the *Boxed In* novels and novellas, interconnecting lives build into a fascinating interplay of human choices and intersecting circumstances.

SLINGS & ARROWS

The events of Slings and Arrows take place some three years before Josie Tasker's life is turned upside down by the events in Outrageous Fortune.

She has retreated from paparazzi intrusion and is living a quiet life. She is in her mid-thirties, financially secure, has a wonderful home and good friends – but she reaches a personal crossroads and decides to plunge back into her career. She has the offer of work and romance is in the air – but then a stalker appears and bitter threats overshadow the promise of love.

Can Josie survive these Slings and Arrows?

OUTRAGEOUS FORTUNE

Since fortune first smiled on Josie Tasker, her life as a singer turned actress has become such as dreams are made of. Then she turns forty, and a series of disasters strip Josie of everything.

Does outrageous fortune favour the brave, the rogue or the saint? As Josie negotiates her maze of misfortune she discovers her real friends, a new life and unexpected love.

Outrageous Fortune can be read and enjoyed as an entirely secular, contemporary romance, understood as a very positive journey through loss, or appreciated as an analogy of the well-known Old Testament story on which it is based. However it is read, it is an affirming story of love.

TO THE THIRD GENERATION

Sarah Price is one of life's copers – but when her husband falls in love with another man, her marriage falls apart and so does she. Determined to do her best for her children she seeks help from a counsellor but, as she unravels her past, she uncovers a dark family secret that threatens everything she holds dear.

To the Third Generation, the third novel in the Boxed In series, is poignant, romantic and deeply moving.

SOUL TO SOUL

On what turns out to be an ill-fated business trip, Bella is grateful to find a seat on a crowded train. She is keen to avoid male attention but when she meets an old friend she changes her mind. Although neither of them can remember where they last met, however hard they try, it becomes a chance encounter that changes both of their lives...

Soul to Soul is a novella which can be easily read in one sitting.

TURN AROUND TWICE

Hereseth, a tight-knit fishing community in the Highlands of Scotland, is Ruth's home. New families rarely move in and when the King family arrives, every tongue in the town begins to wag. Ruth, though, is captivated by Marlon...

As she grows up, her future seems secure, but her trials and tribulations demand hard decisions and tough choices. Life can change all too quickly – as Mrs King is wont to say: 'Before you can turn around twice and tap your head.'

Turn Around Twice can be enjoyed as a contemporary romance, appreciated as one woman's journey through the changes and chances of life or understood as a retelling of a widely-loved Old Testament story. However it is read, it is a heart-warming story of hope.

Parbar Publishing

Parbar Publishing is a small,
independent publishing company
based in the North of England.

Parbar books include:

Adult fiction

Children's fiction

Poetry & Pictures

Christian non-fiction

www.parbarpublishing.com

Facebook